WYATT AT THE COYOTE PALACE

KRISTIN HERSH

WYATT AT THE COYOTE PALACE

KRISTIN HERSH

CREDITS

Produced by Kristin Hersh & Steve Rizzo
Recorded and mastered by Steve Rizzo at Stable Sound Studio in Portsmouth, RI
Vocals & instruments by Kristin Hersh

All songs written by Kristin Hersh
Published by Yes Dear Music, BMI
Administered by BMG Music worldwide except Mushroom Music (Aust./NZ)

Art direction & design by David Narcizo / lakunadesign.com
Photographs & essays by Kristin Hersh

Business Management: Geoff Trump
webmaster: Tine Hughes

kristinhersh.com

This edition published by Omnibus Press and distributed in the United States and Canada by
The Overlook Press, Peter Mayer Publishers Inc, 141 Wooster Street, New York, NY 10012
For bulk and special sales requests, please contact sales@overlookny.com or write to us
at the above address.

Copyright © 2016 Omnibus Press
(A Division of Music Sales Limited)
14/15 Berners Street,
London, W1T 3LJ, UK.

Cover & book design by Dave Narcizo / lakunadesign.com
Photographs by Kristin Hersh

ISBN 978-1-4683-1381-9

Printed in China.

A catalogue record for this book is available from the British Library.

Cataloguing-in-Publication data is available from the Library of Congress.

Visit Omnibus Press on the web at www.omnibuspress.com

bright 10

bubble net................................. 13

in stitches................................. 15

secret codes............................. 17

green screen 20

hemingway's tell....................... 21

detox.. 22

wonderland 25

WYATT AT THE COYOTE PALACE

KRISTIN HERSH

day 3 27

diving bell................................. 29

killing two birds........................ 30

guadalupe 34

august 35

american copper....................... 36

some dumb runaway 39

sun blown 41

from the plane.......................... 44

elysian fields............................. 46

soma gone slapstick 48

cooties 50

christmas underground 50

between piety and desire 52

shaky blue can.......................... 55

shotgun..................................... 56

strange angels.......................... 62

"How many times would you say you guys've almost died?"

"Well not *died* exactly, just had stuff fall on us, fell offa things, wandered into earthquakes, fires, floods or … you know, limbs falling off, shit like that. How many times? I dunno. Never counted."

"It's just that the way you tell it, it seems like a lot. Limbs falling off?"

"I put it back on. *Could* be a lot. And I never even told you about the times that weren't funny. I only tell you the stories."

"I bet almost-deaths happen all the time but we don't even notice. And I would imagine … *most* almost-deaths are funny. Cuz a respectable disease isn't gonna just land on you all of a sudden like a Looney Tunes safe."

"Huh. So we just … wander around poking forks into things 'til we bump into a toaster?"

"Yeah. The fork is a question mark, the toaster is the answer. Or the act of god equivalent."

"I totally blame god. And his acts."

"Well, he's obviously been after you for a very long time."

bright

keep your head, dumbass

it won't last

keep your head down and follow the hood

georgia's gentle pills should sell jokes for the slo-mo

water for the wicked

and love for the lonely

cold sheets

hot night

heavy tries hurling us back into the bright

road coat

road map

a road cold

hot pillows sticky with something

what was that awful drink?

what was that cheerleader drink for the wicked?

and love for the lonely

cold feet

hot light

heavy tries hurling us back into the bright

...

Drugs are adhesives. The word 'high' never made sense to me when it referred to landing our clay here on this plane heavily, with a *whoosh*. Sort of celebrating its sensitivities. In health class, they told us not to drink on an empty stomach or the alcohol might make us drunk. Lesson learned: always drink on an empty stomach. Calls off your censors.

Those goddamn censors, gagging us.

Pulling into a driveway in the middle of the night, we're offered cheerleader drinks and unholy pills. One of us takes a pill with a gulp of goo and wakes with twice the tongue and an aversion to cheerleaders that never really fades.

Post-root canal, we read the bottle of painkillers carefully and follow the contraindicated directions, take them with a fishbowl of wine. On an empty stomach. And with whatever we have around the house to get us where we're going. Post-shaky badness, we do worse. Post-waking nightmare and you place one foot on the other side: do the heaven hokey-pokey. *High?* More like skimming the depths of brackish dream water, skate-like. You go deep enough and caregivers' faces press into yours, your eyes crossing in confusion, trying to focus. "What did you take and how much?" *Not nearly enough.*

Or it isn't chemistry but life that knocks you down. Not all the *way* down. All the way down isn't life's job, it's death's. If your heart is beating, your lungs expanding and contracting, well maybe death didn't *do* its job. But life is not yet your friend. Your only friend is the caregiver in front of you and you only feel their touch, hear their voice. "Where does it hurt and how much?"

Pain is a grinding restlessness. Back up to the surface, bending with the bends, twisted out of your skate form, riding on a human spine again. *Show some backbone.*

Nurse Nadine, with a syringe of Dilaudid: "You got six stab wounds in a pretty circle. Breathe, baby, it won't hurt forever."

bubble net

inspired weakness under sleepy sun

and one cloud is a meltdown

there's no tomorrow

bang a left

a bubble net waits over the next plateau

wearing tear stains

hovering over your shame

syringes scatter below

your body freight

baptize your weight

let it go past the next threshold

there's no tomorrow

...

"Does altering your chemistry put you in limbo? Closer to dead?

"I dunno. Whadda *you* think?"

"Any altered state is an in-between..."

"Watching *cartoons* is an altered state."

"So's slow motion, have you noticed?"

"Way. Once, my kids and I were standing on a street looking into the window of a costume store near a club I was playing. The store was closed, but there we all these dead clowns hanging in the window, so we were staring at 'em."

"Dead clowns?"

"Fake ones. Then we got bored, and while we were climbing back onto the tour bus, a car screeched up onto the sidewalk, ran into another car, killed the driver and smashed into the window of the costume shop. Killed the dead clowns, too."

"Wow. You guys coulda died, too."

"We coulda died even more than *that* cuz the driver's alive, somehow, and he's like, a fugitive, the cops are chasing him. So he gets outta the car and runs toward the bus, while the cops're *shooting...*"

"Holy shit."

"I pushed all my kids down on the floor and we crawled to the back of the bus. In *slow motion.*"

"See? And what were you thinking?"

"That it seemed like a nice town, maybe we should settle down there. Whatta you *mean* what was I thinking? I was thinking I shoulda been a mailman."

"But ... one foot in heaven?"

"Lying on the floor, my arms around my babies. So slow that it all stops. No tomorrow."

"Yeah. I like that."

in stitches

slink past the stoned rasta painters on baronne

blink and the walmart of the dead blurs on baronne

found you

look around you

wild parrots and gin in the air

don't know where to go

don't know where to go from here

don't know where to go to disappear

tangerine and seasick green

us in pieces

like when wolverine

big red's king

caught us hiding

we just drove away into the day

in stitches

...

If you stay on the floor, though? I mean, if you find yourself hiding cuz you don't know where to turn, where to go, maybe you should find a way to disappear. But first, try throwing down your arms. Whatever guns you thought you were hiding clatter to the floor, go off impotently. No enemies around; they were made up, as it turns out. *Hallelujah.*

Walking past the Walmart of the Dead - the only City of the Dead in New Orleans with dusty merchandise crammed between the graves - waving to the stoned painters who once gave us a stone fish. Parrots fly overhead and gin clouds and drums waft out an open window. We need no weapons.

Then far, far away, on Big Red, the big, red tour bus, always raining. Clambering past beloved knees, grabbing a beer and a glimpse of the English countryside, spilling the beer when I try to open it on the edge of a rickety table. *What is this shit? Balsa wood?* Our bus driver, Wolverine, self-described king of his domain: Big Red. Wolverine and his kitten calendars add a touch of bizarre to what should be mundane by now. That's a good thing. We still need no weapons.

Then load-in, in a now catastrophic rain, hauling gear up flights of stairs to the stage and back out into the rain pain.

Of course, my guitar is electric, plugged into an amplifier, plugged into a dirty outlet, and as my soaking wet lips brush the microphone, they're blown off my face in a spray of sparks. Or they would've been had I been able to remain standing. Instead, I fell backward, not a thought in my buzzing brain, blood pouring out of my laughing mouth.

"Kris. You are fucking retarded."

I sat up, still gripping my guitar with soaking wet fingers and wiping the blood off my chin with the other hand. *I know, I know, I know.*

secret codes

woke up wide awake and prayed

sorta know how to pray

you just ache with hope 'til it goes away

you only know secret codes

to god and man you only know secret codes

you're terra firma on singapore air

you're bouncing babies when we had no fear

flat on a bare mattress

then you disappear

adrenaline again

caffeine and palsied balls

you're just greasing up lightning

you don't need my help at all

just ache with hope 'til it goes away

you only know secret codes

…

"Kris, you *are* fucking retarded. That's just … stupid."

"I know, that's why it's funny."

"But entirely avoidable."

"Not really. I had to work and I was wet. I get shocked all the time. There was this cattle fence between my house and the studio last winter? Farmhouse out in the … you know, farmland. And I got *tasered* on the cow fence every goddamn time I walked home from a session. Two a.m. and I'm on the ground making snow angels all o' the sudden and I don't know why. I weigh much less than a cow."

"Huh."

"A shock does weird shit to your heart, too. It stops then races."

"Are you speaking metaphorically?"

"I never speak metaphorically. You don't have to. Anywayz, adrenaline knocked entire days outta my head. True story."

"Your truth doesn't make sense."

"It makes sense."

"To *you* maybe."

"It's the *truth*."

"In code."

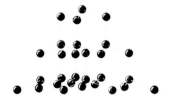

green screen

stuck in his thumb

pulled out a plum

frightened miss muffet away

token sad freak

on a bad beach

sun burns sunburn

under your thumb

red skin blackening

what is happening?

the art of kissing

the heart of missing you

...

No humans on this beach, no people for miles and miles.

The painkillers and the pain are fighting and I'm losing. A barnacle on a mussel, inches from my face, comes in and out of focus. I'm lying on a rock, can see the sky, know my sunburn is soaking up more sunshine, reddening, then blackening. Last thing I looked at and *saw* was my guitar case, *The Art of Kissing* lying in it, sidewise. Then my head lolls and the blue sky becomes gray rock, gray rock becomes red eyes and then I'm not a me anymore. Passed the fuck out, of all things.

Tides come in, then recede, and take whatever they find on the beach with them. Today, it's my dumb little body, floating out with the seaweed and beer cans, bumping along under the bridge like a fallen seagull: clunky, dirty. The passed out are not good swimmers. I wake up already paddling, though, so I guess they aren't *non*-swimmers.

hemingway's tell

love these swastika trees

and spitting in the wind

cold war, hot war, peace

another lesson we don't need

swimming to normal

hemingway's tell: sweet fear

spark meet gasoline and bitchy oxygen

halfway down the rock

shatter my fingers and my heart

another ending we won't start

...

"How come you didn't drown?"

"Because I didn't. What do you mean?"

"The water woke you up?"

"Swimming woke me up. Brought me back to normal. Swimming in my sleep."

"That happens?"

"Not often."

detox

circumlocution

just a parlor game in a kissing chair

anything to make me sigh

you never really changed

you never really tried to detox

a constellation of zits and a snail trail of snot

i'm losing patience with this

hoping that you're not an asshole

echo location

i owned those ugly streets and that ugly man by walking all over them

by being other than

i never really tried to detox

a dire harbinger

fire engine red

what holds your cells together?

will or just a killer's fear of death?

that ugly mouth

a freakish holdout

thought you were used to it

forgot to choose this shit

a holy constellation and you abused it

a snowy haunted season shining up your shoes

bet that's the only reason you don't lose

self immolation

just a parlor game in a kissing chair

anything to make me laugh

...

It hadn't rained in forever. LA isn't generous with rain. We felt dirty inside and out. *Gotta get clean.* So we made detoxing gazpacho. A craving we picked up from Almodovar and couldn't quell with the salad-in-a-blender we found in LA restaurants. But we weren't personally well-versed in gazpacho. In Spain, they pick up a carton and a tortilla for the train, passing the carton around like a joint, staring out at the white-dry steppe country moving past. That's what we wanted, but our gazpacho had no view, tasted like water, then too much like peppers. He tweaked the recipe, adding wine and olive oil, then salt, making more gazpacho with every tweak.

Undefeated but getting bored, we ran out to Von's for cilantro and red onions. Made *more* gazpacho: garlic, pepper and honey. *Honey? Uh... try it.* Made more freakin' gazpacho. Lime. Some more limes. Until we'd filled every vessel in the apartment with fibrous, reddish goo. It looked like the roof was leaking soup.

We didn't even want it anymore, so we opened the door and dragged the dripping vessels into the hallway where the hookers hung out. 'Models' they called themselves. Anyway, they brought their own bowls and spoons to the gazpacho party and we used coffee mugs as ladles, the women laughing, eating and nodding; wide-eyed with their big ol' false eyelashes. Cheap bikinis. Glittery.

We decided our gazpacho must not suck so bad, if we were cleaning our neighbors, who shoulda been clean and weren't allowed to be. So we sunk to the floor, had some ourselves. Detoxing in the moldy, shaded hall, a dry wind sucking past the apartment doors, past the sad plants and sadder ladies.

hooker gazpacho

tomatoes (tons)

some cucumbers

fewer bell peppers than you'd think, and make 'em red, orange or yellow ones

more chili peppers than you want (trust me)

honey

wine

cilantro

garlic

a red onion

olive oil

limes, limes, and more limes

stale bread

salt and pepper

Put it all in a blender and pulverize it. Eat in a drafty hallway.

wonderland

you said aloud: "i'm not allowed, i'm in trouble, i'm in trouble"

under your breath: "i got one left in me, i'm in trouble"

you step outside and hydrogen pops again on the white hot sidewalk

thunder and wonderland gone

you got it backwards

thunder and wonderland gone

you had it all

you're losing her

losing

you're lost

you run and hide

you're losing her

losing

you're lost

...

"That's not a brush with death."

"Nope. That happened later."

"Yeah?"

"Rain dance. A rain dance that worked. It rained, anyway. Thunder and lightning over the pool in the courtyard of our apartment building. Rare in an LA summer."

"And you were in the pool?"

"It was hot. A heat wave. Hot rain. The sidewalk was popping, white explosions, like hydrogen in the air, I swear to god. It was a crazy summer."

"Dumbass."

"You couldn't stand on the sidewalk in bare feet, so we wore shoes up to the edge of the pool and jumped in. Then the soles of our shoes melted, adhered to the pool deck."

"In the electrical storm."

"Thunder and lightning and hot water didn't cool it off any."

"Huh. I wonder how often dumbass causes death."

"Probly don't wanna know. Death loses some drama when you add *dumbass* to it. But the white hot day became a dark and stormy night and that was ... well, it was cool. It woulda been okay if we got struck by lightning. Geez, I mean, struck by lightning: that's an honor."

day 3

melting into slo-mo

an inevitable slowing

weak in the knees and in the fists

all signs waiting patiently for you to spot them pointing

and your e.s.p. is on the fritz

day 3

christen this city with the sound you grew up wanting

jangle trauma in the light

bus stop junkies looking pretty as the morning

jungle hot after a rainy night

day 3

and by dawn we're floating, flying

and by dawn we're neurons firing

...

Another dark and stormy summer night, years later, in New Orleans. Brighter than light lightning flashes turned the yard a cold robin's egg blue, thunder shaking the goddamn roof off. At three in the morning, I opened my eyes and saw the silhouette of a man in the bedroom doorway. Big guy. I wanna say huge, cuz he looked huge, but ... I don't wanna exaggerate. He might've just been big. But I think he was huge.

So I thought: *hello, death.* And the opposite of fight-or-flight kicked in: going limp like a wild animal. Weak kneed, fingers not forming into fists, but hanging loose to calm the sheets. Figured the next sound I heard was gonna be gunshots. *This is New Orleans, after all; it's about time we got shot. We'll be dead before dawn.* Strange.

I was cool with it. Slow motion, no motion, makes you cool with anything. But the guy didn't move, didn't shoot, just stood in the doorway. I waited, squinting into the dark. Couldn't see his features, so I sat up in bed to get a look at him in the robin's egg light. Saw him looking at *me* in the robin's egg light. Then he cleared his throat and said carefully, *"Emily Lauer?"*

diving bell

on the way

you blab like a happy bimbo

sifting the night air for weapons before you suck it into your lungs

into the diving bell with foraging behemoths

to a snow-blown motel and beachcombing behemoths

on the way

you blush like a raving psycho

tossing a mussel back to life

before you suck us into your eyes

into the diving bell

favoring my bad leg

to a snow-blown motel

i'm dragging my bad leg

the horizon's heaven's assault

you can live on the salt

you can live on it all

...

"He said what?"

"Emily Lauer."

"Why?"

"He thought I was Emily Lauer. I guess the girl who rented the apartment before us, who gave him a key."

"Well, then, that's not a brush with death, either."

"No, I just thought it was. So did the *guy*, cuz when my husband woke up, he went psycho, pretended to have a gun. Chased him outta the apartment with an invisible gun. And some invisible dogs, I think, even though we had *visible* dogs. Who just weren't doing anything. I dunno, I was laughing pretty hard."

"Going psycho was taking care of you."

"Yeah, his deal was: us not dying."

"You could live on not dying."

"It's true, you could."

killing two birds

street puke's not your fault

just walk by it

remember coke falls when it all stopped shining?

when the snow stopped falling

you're my nightmare in shining armor

static in the air

everyone like me's a dead man

everyone like me's a dead man

hold on

i'll buy this in a caffeinated moment

killing two birds with one stone

kissing in a bad rain and exhaust

could be worse, ms. hersh, you know where you are

could be worse, ms. hersh, you could be lost

numb means nothing hurts me anymore

and i can't feel a thing in my core

i can't feel a thing anymore

i lose you in the street puke and the rain

and if it's not my fault how come i'm dirty?

i'm so hungover, i'm ashamed

killing two birds with one stone

it's 3:59

and the buzz drills a song home

clean, you dream clean

everyone like me's a nightmare

everyone like me's a nightmare

...

Sixteen, pumped full of cocaine, bad choices and worse friends, driving until my car couldn't move me fast enough, the grey of afternoon settling into a creepy purple evening. On the island where I grew up, people smoke pot in the winter and do coke in the summer. This summer evening was stretching out in all directions over the ocean, looking to be a long one.

I pulled the car over, slammed the door shut and began to run. Almost immediately, a car slowed next to me. I recognized the driver as a friend from high school. "Kris?"

I kept running. "Yeah?"

"Watcha doin'?"

"Coke."

"Uh-huh. How you feeling?"

I glanced at her, kept running. Her car crept along, keeping pace with me. "Just a little irritable, edgy, you know." She watched me run, waiting for more. "Kinda heart attacky."

"Tightness in the chest?" she asked casually. "Difficulty breathing? Numbness down your left arm?" I nodded. "Right. How 'bout you get in and we'll go to the hospital?"

"Nah...it'll go away."

"Would you like to run alongside the car to the hospital?" she offered. I took off my t-shirt and threw it on the grass, kept running. "Nope."

"Honey, you're taking off your clothes."

"Not *all* of them," I answered, annoyed. "It's hot."

"Hold on," she said and suddenly, a wave of nausea had me bent over in the street. My friend pulled over, got out of her car and leaned against the hood, sighing as she watched me puke.

"It's not gonna snow for a long, long time," she reflected.

guadalupe

inside the winter palace

crummy summer haze

the whole place yellow

trouble and disappointment have come to me

help me, our lady guadalupe

help me

...

"You have nice friends. Glad you shook off the bad ones."

"I think about her every time I walk past street puke here in
New Orleans."

"Which is … a lot."

"Which is a lot."

"Hope you don't tell her that she reminds you of street puke."

"No, I'm a nice friend, too."

"Why did she want it to snow?"

"It was a coke joke, like summer snow, but also cuz in winter, is-
landers smoke pot and stop having heart attacks. And because snow
is clean. Sometimes it's hard to watch loud summer come to a quiet
winter place. Trouble is troubling then, nowhere to hide … sunlight
shining on everything. Last summer was a hard one. I climbed into a

friend's dark attic, curled up on a futon and lit an our Lady of Guada-lupe candle; prayed for help until it snowed again."

"Guadalupe takes care of you?"

"Mmmmmaybe."

august

it's all saltwater these days:
ocean, tears and heartbreak soup
half alive in a whitecap foam
half in love with a white half moon

this is my stop
i'm getting off
this is my stop

...

Or you could dive into saltwater. That resonates, works like a solvent, like soap. Ocean, tears and heartbreak soup all have basically the same ingredients. Ask the surfers.

Add a trace mineral infusion, underwater, but also whipping past your ears at the beach; mist and sand press into your skin, work their way into your bloodstream, change you. Fry in the air, blank-eyed seagulls. Can they help you stick around? I dunno. Changes you. You become sand, a pillar of salt, Lot's wife. So I guess not.

Deserts do this too, oddly. You can *hear* minerals in the wind, I swear. I know that sounds stupid, but it's true. Strange sounds in the desert.

Suddenly a dozen coyotes'd yip and wail at exactly midnight. An owl, who wanted to eat our dog, moaned like a bass flute. A drum circle on our front porch cuz hippies never know when to go home. They serenaded us to sleep.

In the morning, Western jays screeched into my window; one with half a beak watching me shower cuz he had to be a fighter and wanted to be the first bird to breakfast. Which those birds shoulda been more grateful for, really. I felt like Snow White out there in the dusty sun, whipping birdseed around in a spiral, but I got the feeling the jays thought they were fighting me for my seeds and winning.

Once, a roaring wall of fire raced across the desert, burned everything but the wild buckwheat and some jackrabbits, who then ate the buckwheat. Blew up the juniper bush outside our kitchen window. I imagine it smelled like burnt gin, but I could actually be imagining that.

american copper

american copper
when you're under
breathe

no little thing i say
no little thing i do
when pieces of us were the same
you went sanpaku

the secret was in your face
it's gone
you're gone, too

say you're foaming

break with the moment

and sleep

...

"You swim with alligators."

"Very small alligators."

"You pick up every snake you see."

"Yeah, which is like … hundreds of snakes. Never been bit once. They go limp in my hands cuz I'm so boring. I bore them to comatose. Pet a wild wallaby once."

"Did it bite you?"

"No. Got two black widow bites, though."

"Did *they* kill you?"

"Nope. Made me a little dizzy, that's it. Killer bees."

"Nuh-uh."

"Yuh-huh. In our house. And killer honey under the floorboards."

"...earthquakes?"

"*Tons.* Soothing rumbling, like Magic Fingers. Dishes'd clatter, a really pretty sound. But the 6.8 in Seattle? Dear lord. Lake Washington was foaming."

"Cool."

some dumb runaway

our crummy commie neighbors draw the blinds on gutter pissing

by midnight

hard to tell when they've had enough

doubling up on every vice

i'm doubled over on my knees again

only way i know how to be

i just adopted your thing about hope as doubt

some dork horked his rolling rock

skidded, hit a kid on the sidewalk

hard to tell when we've had enough

the stars align so drink up

don't have much pull miles away

some dumb runaway

waiting for the moon

better spit out that bad voodoo

now under this streetlight

screw the moon

...

The normally sweet, steady lake looked like a tablecloth being shaken out: waves that extended onto the land, a waterbed motion, trees bending fantastically. Our house took the same waves, undulating, cracking and moaning. Normally, you only see waves affect water, but these waves were not confined to the lake.

I raced down the stairs, frantic, looking for the baby, grabbed an older son and placed him in a doorway. Out of the corner of my eye, through a window, I saw a man who'd been pruning a tree grip a branch as it swung up and down. He was laughing. He didn't fall. I know a woman who fell out of a tree and lost her sense of smell. I know a man who fell from grace and lost his heart. Bad voodoo.

I knew a kid who said he stopped seeing the moon. That it went away. He didn't bother to look up at night maybe, or always at the wrong time, in the wrong part of the sky, at clouds, I dunno. He died, too, without ever seeing it again. You can lose anything, it seems. They don't tell you this when you're born, but you have to hold onto your moon or you don't get to keep it. You have to hold onto your anything or be willing to lose it, to let it go. It's your choice, I guess. This guy in the tree with the pruning shears waving dangerously near his face? He held on.

Like dream swimming in the air, I teetered from floor to floor, counting children.

During the aftershocks, our neighbors all gathered under a streetlight, helping each other breathe. They apologized to us, for some reason. They were laughing, too, just like the guy in the tree. They'd held on.

sun blown

where you gotta go?

where do you come from?

ask me no questions

i'll tell you no lies

i'm still fucking fried post-ablutions and plane drain

tell me no secrets

i'll tell you no lies

i'm so fucking tired of dissolution

the bailing mate dance

failing patience

fool's silver sun blown

fool's aluminum

rats from a sinking ship we run for the trees

the blast comes and shit you took all there was to breathe

you pasted something to my head

blundering and blindfolded

alone, cold, on the road

i got nowhere to go

i was holding you under your headlamp hatred

and when you looked down i melted

i was holding you under

your eyes full of hatred

and when you looked up i melted

...

"Car crashes?"

"Just one. Lost a leg, put it back on. But the *bus* crash: that was nuts. We had to get to the next show in Minneapolis, we were coming from, uh … somewhere else. A mountain road, winding around and around. Lost power steering, the bus filled with smoke, flames in the back where one of our sons was. I handed the baby to my drummer cuz he's big and strong and tour buses don't have seat belts. Then my bass player and I ran back to get one of the other boys. My husband was yelling, 'Don't go back there!' But he didn't know one of our kids was back there. You know, where the flames and smoke were coming from."

"Jesus."

"Jesus wasn't there until later. First, we had to crash in the woods and go hungry and get dirty for a few days. We waited to be rescued, I cut my hair off in the dark, crooked bathroom of the bus. Nobody rescued us. So I told my bandmates I'd cancel the rest of the tour and use the last of my savings to fly them home. They just shook their heads. Hungry and dirty, remember, exhausted; they group hugged me with my homemade haircut, said they'd finish the tour no matter what, no matter how, no matter how bad it got.

I mean, the kids were crying; that bus was their only home. My career was over as far as I knew. But who does what my bandmates did? Who gives *themselves?* Who is still a goddamn hero? After all I'd put them through. We hiked to some country store, found a phone, split a cab and a hotel room, told our listeners that this was the end and … you know, *sayonara*."

"Is that when Jesus came?"

"Either Jesus or Frank Capra, yeah."

"Frank Zappa?"

"Frank *Capra.* Maybe Frank Zappa, I dunno. But it was my *It's a Wonderful Life* moment. People rescued us, sent us love notes and money to rent cars and finish the tour, get the bus fixed, you know … eat."

"Wowee."

"My son, Wyatt, says, *when the unthinkable happens, we die: we cross a threshold and start a new life.* So it's like the end of the world is around every corner and a new world is around the next. We weren't coming from anywhere and we weren't going to Minneapolis, we were coming from home and we made it home, even thought we have no home."

"Okay."

"Homeless made me a little hard once. Love melted me."

from the plane

your city looks like campfires from the plane

lite brite cave paintings

dark blue arteries

ice swirls feathering from the plane

you've got ice feather windows

i give

what a nice gesture

though short-lived

spooning sadly

a heart shake

head skipped a beat

...

You came to see us in the Catskills one winter, when we lived on
a frozen lake. Sounded fun, I know, was actually really boring. We
didn't even own a TV. We lived on vodka tonics and chicken wings.
Would've eaten trail mix but the mice kept putting it in our shoes.
By the second afternoon, you had that bored-to-crazed look on your
face, your unibrow permanently raised. Told me spiders were building
webs to trap you in your armchair and that it was time to go outside
and explore snow. "It's white," I told you, "and cold." You smirked
and grabbed a pair of ice skates from the front closet, went out on
the lake. I had told you that ice skating was "easier then it looks" but
through the window, I saw you making it look much harder than it

is. Your ankles were on backwards, your feet flopping around, as you fell again and again, spinning back to the frozen dirt on the shore. I cringed and turned away from the window. A few minutes later, you came tumbling inside, breathless: "Ice skating is *really* hard!" I noticed your skates were untied, told you to hold still and tied them for you, then joined you on the ice.

Slipping over frozen ripples, I grabbed your mittened hand when you spun and we sort of … walked the lake. Because it was me and you, though, we weren't really aware of where we were, or the white cold, because we were talking about music. The conversation we've been having since we were eight years old just loses us. Gets us lost, I mean. Usually, we cut the engine at a stoplight and opened a map, but today, we were in the center of a frozen lake. So we stopped, feverishly expounding on what making sound does to the human heart muscle—you challenging God to sling one more fucking arrow in our direction—when we heard a rifle shot. "Damn, they're shooting bears again," I said, peering into the woods.

You were looking down at the ice. "No they aren't." A narrow, white line crawled between our feet, separating us. The ice was cracking. You bit your lip to keep from smiling.

I could hardly talk, though, I was laughing so hard. *What a way to go.* "Dang, you *fuck*-head. Had to go and challenge God, didn't you? You know how pissed he gets. We're gonna slide under the freakin' ice now and our bodies won't be found 'til spring thaw."

You started skate-running, which is like talk-singing: worse than either activity on its own, just goofiness. I laughed harder, skated faster, and the white line followed us home, winding its way between the feathering ice swirls.

elysian fields

morning

how's the air on mars?

could you sleep hard and hungry, empty?

falling so far

you think you can't last long

tell me, what future were you counting on?

i'm heading back to the ocean

you're hailing a cab in a cold sweat

don't get choked by your deprivation

deprived of what's the question

enough's your destination, right?

way down in elysian fields hoping we'll dream a way out

...

"If you fall through the ice, do you freeze or drown first?"

"Sometimes hypothermia *keeps* you alive. Can't be fun, though."

"Drowning is supposed to be nice."

"I've heard that. I almost drowned at Zuma beach and that was pretty nice. Got calm, dreamy. Dreamed my way out. I didn't flail … the ocean flailed for me."

"If you're dreamy, you probly let the ocean take you. Flailing is for people who haven't had enough life yet, so they feel deprived. They were counting on more and the water's taking their more away. "

*"Flail...*good word."

soma gone slapstick

he wanted palms

secular psalms

"i'll find you a palm tree, make you think you're in california"

clear lungs

clear lust

soma gone slapstick

you leave only footslips

we all hear the same sound

this whole fall on the rebound

find you smoke: nola snow

and we're back in chicago when i jump out the window

your mirror eyes reflecting sky

i did feel sorry for you, overwrought and see-through

a glimmer of the future made this winter even crueler

did you, did you know I feel the same?

can you, can you stomach this old dopey game?

a buzzing like a panic

made this whole spring kinda manic

...

In a midnight parking lot, I got a hint of how troubled you might be. Another midnight in a bright dressing room, I saw how dark you really were. Felt for you. Saw my own darkness reflected in your mirror eyes and it was infinite. The night ended in a fuzzy, stumbling escape. I wanted to take you to California, where you'd be happy, clean, and gentle.

A few hours later, outside our fifth floor hotel window, I weighed the memories I wanted to lose against the ones that hadn't happened yet. Those were kind of a toss up. Was freedom splattered on the Chicago sidewalk or splayed on the hotel room carpet? Was California pretend?

Nurse Nadine: "You ain't got nobody, do you, baby? You ain't got nobody."

cooties

just had to know why you're still terrified

cooties aside

the buzz dies down

all the way down

just had to know if you feel seasick

you look different

we're coming down

all the way down

...

"Do you come down by falling? Fast? Floating gently to the ground and landing in heaven? Or do you step off the window sill, come down to the floor and let yourself off that hook for a minute ... you know, wake up to cereal and TV again?"

"Yeah. Where does it hurt?"

christmas underground

phony vines crawl through

swamp-sticky flowered and blue

i'll be there, taped it to my fridge

i'm moved

i won't forget you shaking in your boots

but i don't think you can take this anymore

"grey goose'll fake you out
herra dura's gonna melt you down"

i don't wanna let you spill out
degrading's degrading all around

look at you falling around
aw, poor kid's gonna drown
flowers floating in the punch
i ask you what the hell you've done
you're shaking in your boots
well, i don't think you can take this anymore

christmas underground
my hand still bandaged but sound

...

Blue, plastic flowers, as big as your face, wound through a chain link fence, sweaty. And an invitation to a dealie in the desert, a dusty bright night. Punchbowls, blue flowers as big as faces, floating in the pink, swamp coolers spraying it all down with mist.

Cut to: his shaky heart, shaking all the way down to his boots. Eyes jumping, pupils dilated. *What have you done?* Pouring a Grey Goose vodka for me, Herra Dura tequila for him. A friend tells us that the alcohol in our glasses is lying to us. Strange to hear from a man who sucked down that particular lie like no one else I ever knew. But he was trying to help.

Years later, *What have you done?* In shock, the gift of numb. Until its strength gives out, its gentle, lying poster curling up at the edges to reveal the true image underneath.

And another friend whispers across the Atlantic, "The pain is lying to you. I promise." Strange to hear when I thought I *was* the pain. But he was trying to help. And strangely, he did. *How did he do that?*

Once, I cut my thumb almost all the way off, trying to slice a piece of bread for one of the kids while looking over my shoulder at the baby. Blood every-fucking-where. A red sinkful, another red sinkful. Bled for months, big dumb bandage sticking up over the guitar neck. Little pain like that? *That* pain is telling the truth.

between piety and desire

incense, strawberry candles and soap

way to butcher a street

there are spells

dizzying spells

you can smell them coming

a torture on the breeze

did you call me?

what did you call me?

trying to turn the other cheek

all clean junkies miss dirty secrets

we're gonna die so what the fuck

we're only here through sheer dumb luck

and we don't like the shit between piety and desire

no we don't like the shit cuz we belong in it

...

"Hmmmm ... bears? Mountain lions? Rattlesnakes?"

"Well, no. I've *seen* rattlesnakes, in Joshua Tree. They didn't do anything but look at me while I looked at them. Owl Qaeda, though."

"What?"

"Owl Qaeda. Owl attack. Smashed the bus windshield in the middle of the night. We had to drive all night then, so the cops wouldn't see us driving with a broken windshield. We stayed up, made coffee, got giddy."

"Nobody almost died?"

"Nobody but the owl and I think he *did* die. There were sparks."

"Sharks?"

"Sparks."

"No, I mean, shark attacks."

"Oh. No. But we shouldn't have been swimming around covered in blood in goddamn Shark's Cove."

"More stupid."

"Not stupid, ignorant. Got scraped up by coral while we were snorkeling. Didn't know we were in Shark's Cove until waves blew us outta the water."

"You shouldn't have been there."

"You belong everywhere you are, duh-uh. In New Orleans, we lived between Piety Street and Desire Street. Didn't think we belonged *there*, totally did. We're holy and wanting, I guess. Lofty and base."

"You're full of shit."

"Exactly."

shaky blue can

back when everything was gonna be alright

startled in the startling sunshine

tongue-tied

sunshine isn't strychnine

moping in the motel

a shaky blue can

it's your hand shaking

not the can

back when everything was gonna be ok

coping with the motel

we were wide awake

window shade pulled from its frame

sun spilled careless on your careful face

a shaky blue can

it's your hand shaking

not the can

it's not protection but thank you

with diminishing attitude and a sad ineptitude

you loved the unlovable

...

When our plane fell outta the sky over the Alps, we weren't scared, just falling. And fascinated. Air dancing European businessmen, contorting like astronauts; their drinks, in glass glasses—not plastic American ones—smashing on the ceiling, spraying droplets of alcohol into the air. The liquid didn't fall, but the airplane did.

Nothing happens quickly when you're watching. Children grow up in a short time, but the longest short time there is, because we watch, amazed. If we watched all moments as carefully as we watch car crashes, we'd never fuck anything up. Some stuff just doesn't fascinate us enough, I guess. When I was twelve, I pulled a knife on a drunk in the middle of the night to protect my brother and sister. Kicked the guy onto the floor and kept him there at knifepoint while they hid in a bedroom with a chair blocking the door. As drunk as he was, I was the one in slow motion, so I had the upper hand. And the knife. I wasn't brave, just bored and annoyed, but I never forgot the power of slow.

A fever slowed the walls of my hospital room this year. *Slowing a wall* … that's pretty fucking slow. I was packed in ice and getting warmer. Nurse Nadine, chuckling: "One-hundred-and-six. You go, girl. If ice ain't cold any more, you win, baby. You win."

shotgun

i called shotgun

our car submerged

your breakneck speed slowed to a float

out on a thalidomide limb

truncated, stiff as a board

delinquent no more

can't see the fog for the trees

i lost my way on reject beach

lost my heart

lost it

you can't live until you die

i called shotgun

our car submerged

your breakneck speed slowed

two afloat

...

"Floods?"

"Two. In the one where the ceiling collapsed? Our roof caught fire."

"How is that even possible?"

"It's not. But it's true. We just gave up, laughed. Life is ludicrous."

"Huh. Why do we *almost* die? When we're just gonna die later anyway?"

"I dunno. Rehearsal? My son, Bo, tells me that a snake sheds in order to grow. Molting. They'd suffocate if they didn't change bodies and start over. A practice death. Can't live 'til you die. Our lives get itchy, we peel 'em off, start over. Like Wyatt says, crossing a threshold and starting a new life. Same thing."

"Except plus terror."

"The unthinkable. A good death'd maybe be walking away. Wyatt was obsessed with this abandoned building behind my studio called The Coyote Palace. A beautiful thing: clock tower, stables, a wooden fire escape. Completely overgrown, and coyotes live in it with left-behind teapots and mattresses. Wyatt'd flush pink just looking at it, driven to explore. This was before the roof caved in. That's how good a mother I am. Anyway, one day, there was no option of the Coyote Palace any longer. He excised it from his psychology. I think Wyatt wanted to keep it encapsulated as a sense memory, untouchable under the glass of his own filter. I was broken-hearted, but … he could walk away in order to leave the place pristine through his own lens. That's work to me. A work of art."

"Is it love?"

"No, love is forever. Work is a moment. Its forever is in the sharing. But love, work and Wyatt all say, 'I am not special, I am not alone.'"

STRANGE ANGELS
You made this happen. Thank you.

SPONSORS:
Doug Hamilton
Chad Latz
Mrs. Luna Genevieve Martin and
    Mrs. Shannon Marie Martin
Todd Perley
Dan Weissman

EXECUTIVE PRODUCERS:
Paul Bruneau
Paul Dixon
AJ Pym
Francois Wolmarans